I Wonder Why

Volcanoes Blow Their Tops

and Other Questions About Natural Disasters

Rosie Greenwood

KINGFISHER

KINGFISHER
a Houghton Mifflin Company imprint
222 Berkeley Street
Boston, Massachusetts 02116
www.houghtonmifflinbooks.com

First published in 2004
10 9 8 7 6 5 4 3 2 1

1TR/1103/SHE/RBOW/126.6MA

LIBRARY OF CONGRESS CATALOGING-IN-PUBLICATION DATA
Greenwood, Rosie.
    I wonder why volcanoes blow their tops/ Rosie
Greenwood.—1st ed.
        p. cm.
    Includes index
    Summary: Question and answer format provides
scientific information on volcanoes and other
phenomena.
    1. Science—Miscellanea—Juvenile literature. [1.
Science—Miscellanea. 2. Questions and answers.]
I. Title.

Q163.G744 2004
500—dc22   2003061905

ISBN: 0-7534-5751-2

Series designer: David West Children's Books
Author: Rosie Greenwood
Consultant: Keith Lye
Illustrations: Mark Bergin 18bl, Peter Dennis
  (Linda Rogers) 16b; Bill Donohoe 24tl, 25r, 26; James
  Field (SGA) 31; Chris Forsey 4bl, 5, 6–7, 8–9, 12–13
  14–15c, 22–23, 24–25c; Mike Lacey (SGA) 14br, 21,
  24l, 27bl, 29r; Simon Mendez 30–31c; Roger Stewart
  10; Mike Taylor (SGA) 11, 16–17t, 17br, 18–19t, 19b;
  Peter Wilkes (SGA) all cartoons

Printed in Taiwan

CONTENTS

Where does forked lightning come from?

A blinding stream of light zigzags through the sky. This is lightning—a giant electrical spark that begins inside of towering thunderclouds. Lightning heats up the air in its path until it is very hot—hotter than the Sun's surface—and the air explodes in a deafening crash of thunder!

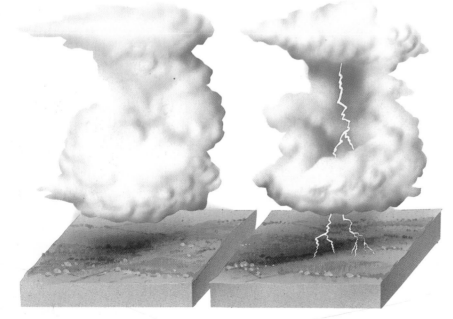

● A thundercloud becomes electrically charged when strong winds toss water droplets, ice crystals, and hailstones up and down inside of it.

● As the water droplets and ice crystals jostle around they generate a huge charge of static electricity. This charge is released in bright flashes of lightning.

● The Vikings believed that lightning was made by the god Thor hurling his hammer, and thunder was the rumble of his chariot's wheels.

● If lightning hits sandy ground, the heat can melt the sand. As it cools into a solid again it forms a glassy sculpture of the lightning flash's path.

What is ball lightning?

Eerie, glowing balls of light are sometimes seen during thunderstorms, floating a short distance above the ground. This spooky effect is called ball lightning. Scientists are not sure what causes it, but the balls might be glowing-hot gases given off when forked lightning strikes the ground.

● Lightning once struck the Empire State Building in New York City 15 times in 15 minutes!

Why do forests catch on fire?

It doesn't take much to start a fire when plants are parched by a hot, rainless summer. A flash of lightning can sometimes spark a dry tree into flames, but most forest fires are caused by people being careless—for example, by throwing away a match that is still lit. Fires can burn through more than one half mile of forest in one hour, and if a fire rages out of control, it can devastate thousands of acres of land.

● Indonesian forest fires raged for months in 1997, creating a choking blanket of smoke over much of Southeast Asia.

● Although forest fires can be damaging, some plants need their help in order to produce new seedlings. Banksias are Australian shrubs whose nutlike seedpods stay tightly shut until they are triggered open by the heat of a bushfire.

Who bombs fires?

In some countries firefighters use a specially designed plane to combat fires. The plane can skim over the surface of a lake or the sea and scoop up hundreds of gallons of water into its tanks. Then the plane flies back to the fire to bomb the flames with its load of water.

● As many as 15,000 bushfires are reported in Australia every year.

How can you fight fire with fire?

A firebreak is a cleared strip of land in front of a fire, where there's no fuel left to feed the flames. Firefighters sometimes set small fires of their own to help clear the ground.

When does a wind become a gale?

The faster the wind blows, the more powerful and dangerous it can be. The Beaufort scale measures wind speed as force 0–12 according to its effect on the surrounding landscape. A gentle breeze is force 3, for example—an 8–12 mph (12–19km/h) wind that rustles twigs. A moderate gale is force 7—a 32–38 mph (50–61km/h) wind that makes whole trees sway!

● Force 10 is a whole gale—a 55–63 mph (89–102km/h) wind that can uproot trees. Storms are force 11, and hurricanes are force 12.

● In March 1993 the eastern coast of Canada and the U.S. was struck by a savage blizzard carried by hurricane-force winds. Thousands of buildings were destroyed or damaged, and the weather was so severe that it was named the "Storm of the Century."

Why are blizzards dangerous?

Freezing-cold winds can whip up the sudden blinding snowstorms that we call blizzards. These can pile up huge snowdrifts, stopping traffic in its tracks and making it impossible for people to go to work or school!

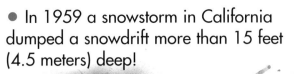

● In 1959 a snowstorm in California dumped a snowdrift more than 15 feet (4.5 meters) deep!

Why did we shoot at clouds?

Hailstones can be the size of baseballs and can cause a lot of damage. In some countries farmers used to try to protect their crops by firing big guns into clouds in order to stop the hail. Scientists are unsure if the guns really worked.

● In Iowa in 1882 two living frogs were found inside of big hailstones! They were probably sucked up by a twister.

How much damage can a hurricane do?

With winds roaring at more than 73 mph (117km/h), hurricanes are the fiercest storms on Earth. They start above warm, tropical seas, and if a severe hurricane reaches land, it can flatten forests, smash houses, flip over cars, and even lift boats out of the water!

● Hurricanes can bring torrential rain and crashing waves and can sweep floods of seawater in over the coast. Once on land the howling winds lose power and quickly die away.

Where is a hurricane's eye?

The eye of a hurricane is a central zone where the wind is fairly calm and there are no big storm clouds. The fast and furious hurricane winds move in a spiral around the eye.

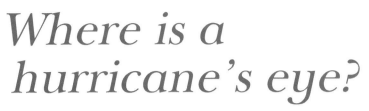

• Each hurricane is given a name. The first one of the year usually begins with A, such as "Hurricane Alice." The second begins with B and so on through the alphabet. Few names begin with the letters Q, U, X, Y, or Z though!

What do hurricanes, typhoons, and cyclones have in common?

They are all words for the same thing—and they all spell trouble! The word "hurricane" is used in North and South America, "typhoon" in the Far East, and "cyclone" in Australia and India.

• Special weather planes help scientists track hurricanes so that they can issue warnings to people.

What wind can sink a ship?

Hurricanes are just as dangerous out at sea as they are on land. Most waves are caused by wind blowing across the water's surface, and a hurricane can whip up a 98-ft. (30-m)-high wall of water. When a freak wave of this size smashes down, it can sink even large ships in minutes.

How do sailors know a storm is on its way?

Scientists use planes, ships, and satellites to keep a close eye on the weather. Information is passed on to the rest of us by TV and radio stations, and sailors make sure they tune in for regular updates.

● Vicious gales and high tides can combine to cause devastating floods in low-lying coastal areas, endangering people and damaging their homes.

Which boats are unsinkable?

Lifeboats race to the rescue during shipwrecks. Modern lifeboats can cope with really wild weather—if a big wave tips one over, it flips right back up!

Why are twisters so dangerous?

"Twister" is a nickname for a tornado, a spinning windstorm that is usually born inside of a huge thundercloud. A tornado snakes down to the ground, sucking up everything in its path. Tornadoes are narrower than hurricanes, but they can be just as destructive.

● The world's worst place for tornadoes is Tornado Alley—a belt of land that stretches across several states between the Rocky Mountains and the Appalachian Mountains, from Minnesota to Texas.

What is a waterspout?

If a tornado forms over a lake or sea, it sucks up water and is called a waterspout. When its winds die down, it can drop its load of water like a bomb.

● If you're ever caught in a shower of fish, it's because a waterspout has sucked them up from a lake or the sea!

Where can you see a devil?

Hot air will sometimes swirl up from dry desert land, carrying dust and sand almost 500 feet (152m) high—this is a dust devil!

Where can wind strip paint off of a car?

When a windstorm blows up in the desert, it blasts sand at anything in its path. Sand can strip the surface off of all types of tough materials—even cars. That's why wood is smoothed with sandpaper and stone is polished with sand-blasting machines!

● A sprinkling of sand from the Sahara desert has been known to fall in Great Britain, thousands of miles away.

What is the Dust Bowl?

The Dust Bowl is a region in the U.S. Midwest whose name dates back to the 1930s. There was so little rain in those years that the soil dried up, turned into dust, and was blown away by windstorms. No crops grew, and farming families had to abandon their land and their homes.

● Ancient rock paintings show that the Sahara desert was once much wetter and greener and that giraffes and elephants grazed there.

How can a child be so destructive?

Warm and cold ocean currents help shape the world's climate. In the Pacific Ocean a cold current called La Niña (Spanish for "the girl") usually flows west from South America to Indonesia. But every three to seven years a warm current called El Niño ("the boy") flows eastward in the opposite direction. Sometimes El Niño is strong, causing disastrous weather, including droughts, hurricanes, and floods, from Alaska to Australia.

● La Niña has the opposite effect to El Niño. In Australia and Indonesia, for example, La Niña brings rain and good conditions for farming.

When does mud slide?

If torrentially heavy rain pelts down onto a steep mountain slope, it can turn loose soil into liquid mud and wash it away. Sometimes a roaring river of mud sweeps down off the mountain, drowning everything in its path.

● The waters rose very quickly when flash floods struck southern Mozambique in February 2000. There was so little time to escape that thousands of people were trapped for days on the roofs of houses and in treetops.

What makes floods happen in a flash?

Flash floods got their name because they happen so quickly. Torrential rain can swamp a river or stream, making it suddenly burst its banks and spill out over the surrounding countryside.

- When a Colombian volcano blew its top in 1985, the heat melted its ice cap and created mudflows called lahars, which buried a whole town.

- Lahars can surge downhill at almost 60 mph (100km/h).

How do floods help us?

When rivers burst their banks, they dump rich mud on the land, which helps farmers grow crops. The ancient Egyptians, for example, built their great civilization on the narrow strip of fertile farming land created by the Nile river flooding every year. The rest of their huge country was made up of dry, dusty deserts.

- Noah's flood may have happened when the Mediterranean Sea broke through a strip of land, turning a freshwater lake into the salty Black Sea.

When does snow race at 190 mph?

Snow can break away from a mountain slope and crash downhill at incredible speeds. This is an avalanche, and it can be triggered by anything from an earthquake to the swish of a skier's skis. The worst avalanches race along as fast as an express train, roaring louder than thousands of lions as they bury houses and villages, railroads and roads.

● Be careful where you yodel in Switzerland—loud noises are another way of setting off an avalanche!

● During World War I soldiers fired their guns to set avalanches off onto their enemies.

Who is an avalanche victim's best friend?

No avalanche rescue team would be complete without its specially trained dogs. With their sharp sense of smell, dogs are excellent at sniffing out people hidden under the snow. And as soon as they find someone, the dogs start digging a rescue tunnel.

What makes land slide?

Disasters, such as avalanches and landslides, are most common in mountainous regions where there are no trees. Trees help keep land safe because they bury their roots down into the ground, anchoring it and stopping it from being swept away.

What happens in an earthquake?

A small earthquake makes the ground tremble. A powerful one makes it shudder and shake like a ship rocking on the ocean and even crack wide open. The most devastating earthquakes can move mountains, make rivers change course, and bring whole cities tumbling down to the ground.

● In Japanese legend earthquakes were triggered by a giant catfish named Namazu wriggling around.

● Earth's solid outer layers are split into gigantic chunks called plates, which float on the partly runny layer beneath. Most earthquakes are caused by the plates bumping and grinding together.

When does soil turn into soup?

In areas with soft, wet soil an earthquake can sometimes make the ground act like it's a liquid. Buildings sink and stay firmly stuck even when the shaking stops and the ground becomes solid again.

How do we measure earthquakes?

An instrument called a seismometer is used to measure the vibrations, or shaking movements, of the ground during an earthquake. In some seismometers a pen records the vibrations on a piece of paper that is wrapped around a turning drum. The pen is attached to a weight and stays still during the earthquake, while the drum bounces around.

● Laser beams are used to measure ground movement and help warn when an earthquake is coming.

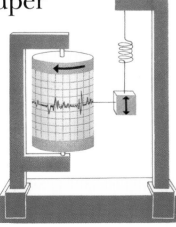

Which mountains spit fire?

If you ever see huge fiery clouds spurting out of a mountain, you can be sure it's a volcano—and what's even worse, it's blowing its top! The most violent volcanoes explode like bombs, spitting out clouds of hot ash, chunks of solid rock, and fountains of the melted rock we call lava.

Why do volcanoes blow their tops?

Deep beneath a violent volcano is a huge chamber. Hot, runny rock and gases build up there until they blast upward under immense pressure through cracks in Earth's crust.

● Scientists who study volcanoes are called volcanologists. The word "volcano" is named after Vulcan, the Roman god of fire

Where can you see rivers of rock?

Sometimes a red-hot river of lava pours
out of a volcano and flows down its sides.
The liquid rock can reach temperatures
of more than 1,832°F (1,000°C)—much hotter
than an oven—and can flow
faster than you can run!

● As if volcanoes weren't
dangerous enough, their
ash clouds can become
electrically charged and
produce lightning!

What is an avalanche of ash?

Volcanic ash can be even more dangerous than lava. Sometimes ash clouds are not thrown up into the air but instead roll down over the sides of a volcano like an avalanche. As they race downhill, these scorching-hot ash clouds burn, boil, or melt everything in their path.

● When Mount Pinatubo in the Philippines erupted in 1991, an avalanche of ash destroyed land as far as 11 miles (18km) away.

● Violent volcanoes can affect Earth's climate by throwing up ash clouds that shut out the Sun's light. The eruption of Indonesia's Mount Tambora in 1815, for example, was followed by worldwide bad weather.

Which volcano buried a Roman town?

When Italy's Mount Vesuvius erupted in August A.D. 79, ash fell like snow over the Roman town of Pompeii, burying it in 20-ft. (6-m)-deep drifts. Then it rained. Afterward the ash set like concrete, freezing the town in time until it was first excavated in the 1860s.

● Despite its chilly name Iceland is a real hot spot with hundreds of volcanoes—lava has even set houses on fire!

How can volcanoes be good for you?

Although volcanic ash can be very destructive, it brings benefits as well. As the ash wears away, it enriches the soil and helps farmers grow bumper harvests.

How big can waves get?

When an average tsunami wave reaches the shore, it rears up into a 66-ft. (20-m)-high monster. But the tallest in modern times was 279 ft. (85m) high—almost as high as the Statue of Liberty in New York City harbor!

● Tsunamis can speed across the ocean at 620 mph (1,000km/h)—as fast as a jet plane!

● A tsunami may have played a major role in the mysteriously sudden end of the Minoan civilization on the Greek island of Crete around 3,500 years ago. Gigantic 130-ft. (40-m)-high waves are thought to have smashed into Crete at that time, wiping out coastal towns and the entire Minoan fleet.

What sets off tsunamis?

Unlike ordinary ocean waves, which are mostly whipped up by the wind blowing over the water's surface, most tsunamis are shocked into life on the ocean floor. Underwater earthquakes, landslides, and volcanic eruptions are all violent enough to kick start a tsunami.

● When a volcano blew the Indonesian island of Krakatau apart in 1883, so much rock was hurled into the sea that tsunami waves were set off. The monster waves even picked up a ship and dumped it in the jungle on the nearby island of Sumatra.

What is dangerous about space rocks?

Earth is under constant attack from space rocks. Most of them are no bigger than a pebble and burn up as they plunge through the air. But every now and then a big rock smashes into the ground and blasts out a hole called a crater.

● Space rocks that hit the ground are called meteorites.

● The largest known meteorite was found in Africa. At 59 tons it weighed more than ten elephants!

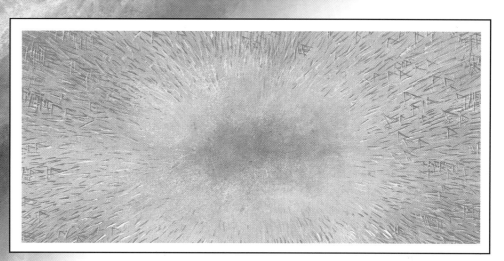

● When a huge space rock exploded high above Siberia in 1908, it flattened a city-sized area of forest on the ground below.

Which was the greatest disaster on Earth?

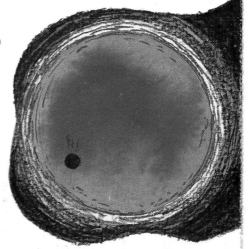

Many scientists think that a giant meteorite strike killed off the dinosaurs 65 million years ago. The blast blew up enough dust to block out the Sun's rays for months. Without sunlight, plants died. Cold and hunger killed the plant-eating dinosaurs first and then the meat eaters.

● One day the Sun will swell into a red giant star and boil away Earth's life-giving water. Don't worry though, this won't happen for another five billion years.

Index